The Confident

Barrel Racer

Disclaimer

This book is for informational and educational purposes. All recommendations are made without guarantee on the part of the author or publisher. The author and publisher shall have neither liability nor responsibility to any person(s) or entity with respect to any loss or damage, caused or alleged to be caused directly or indirectly as a result of the information contained in this book, or appearing on the Barrel Racing Tips.com web site(s). While this book is as accurate as the author can make it, there may be unintentional errors, omissions and inaccuracies.

DEDICATION

To the reader;

May you also, in your own way
dissolve the binding pain of self-doubt
and transform it into freedom
and joy for yourself
and others.

TABLE OF CONTENTS

> *You can be anything you want to be; you can climb any mountain you want to climb; you can reach any goal you want to reach. It all lies within you. Believe in yourself. This can be the year of your dreams, the year of your greatest accomplishments, the year of merited recognition, the year of achieving long-sought mental, spiritual, social, physical and financial goals. And what determines whether or not you make it such a year? It will be if you expect it to be; only if you live with a positive expectancy.*

– Mary Kay Ash

INTRODUCTION

During the first Christmas season my best-selling book, *Secrets to Barrel Racing Success* was available, I wanted to offer a gift to those who purchased it. I thought long and hard about what I could possibly put together as a bonus that would truly reflect my gratitude.

It had to be something that *all barrel racers* would benefit from. I wanted it to be something valuable, something rare, something special, that with my unique combination of experiences, knowledge and skills, would help people in a way that only I could.

Then it came to me – ***CONFIDENCE.***

I often hear from barrel racers from all over the world admitting they struggle with self-doubt. But I know there are *many more* barrel racers that struggle due to a lack of confidence that I never hear from. Of all the positive feedback I've received from *Secrets to Barrel Racing Success*, a fair amount has been regarding the *Inner Game* chapter. Barrel racers continue to thank me for giving them the tools to boost their confidence. I wanted to go *even deeper* in the pages that follow.

Confidence is a subject that's not talked about much other than it being said "You have to be confident!" But what if you're not? And if not, how do you get confident? You certainly don't just buy it at the tack store, or wake up one day a confident barrel  racer and never have another limiting thought (that's not how it happened for me anyway).

Confidence seems hard to find, and it's not something that's very openly talked about, and not something that people (barrel racers especially) tend to jump up and admit they have a problem with. After all, barrel racers are supposed to be tough, strong, capable and fearless, right?

This belief is a big part of *why* barrel racers struggle with confidence issues (more on that in a moment). The truth is that even the highest achieving barrel racer's minds become plagued with self-doubt at times. Honestly, it doesn't matter how much you have already achieved - no one is completely immune to negative self-talk that causes our confidence level to take a plunge. My goal in this guide isn't to help you eradicate those thoughts completely, because that would be unrealistic.

WHY, you say?

Well, maybe you were hoping to never have another questioning or worrisome thought cross your mind. This guide will *not* help you accomplish that, and for good reason. Like horses, humans are also wired in their own way for survival. Our mind's default setting is to see danger - before it kills us. This is why we are so very perceptive to what *we don't want*. We can be thankful for this instinctual tendency, because it's what's responsible for keeping us safe and alive. But because there are no longer saber tooth tigers lurking in the bushes hoping to make us their dinner, this extreme, primal instinct doesn't exactly serve us so well anymore. However, many of us still have the tendency of letting this default setting run amok. Instead of consciously choosing our thoughts, we walk around on auto pilot, allowing fearful thoughts to sink in, and ultimately poison our minds and our lives.

As we get started, keep in mind that it's perfectly normal to experience negative or fearful thoughts from time to time (and that it's not entirely a bad thing). We ALL have thoughts of self-doubt come up now and then, it's when they move into our minds and take up permanent residence that we suffer.

You may have come to a point in your barrel racing journey where you realize that it's your mental game holding you back more than anything else; that there is a direct connection between the quality of your thinking and the quality of your life. I hope you're not willing to be held back any longer. I hope that the time to put your foot down and give confidence busting negative thoughts an eviction notice, is RIGHT NOW.

This guide will explain how that is possible, but *in a way* that you may not have experienced before. I'm *not* going to deliver cold, hard techniques like a sports psychologist, or fill you with a bunch of fluffy psycho-babble, or even give you a firm kick in the rear, in fine barrel racer fashion – I'm going to do **all three of those things** (and more), but *in a unique, integrative way* I feel will serve barrel racers best.

> *"Life doesn't give you dreams and aspirations for you to turn away and say 'not for people like me.' Your dreams are your real self, yearning to be followed with a courageous heart and unbending intent."*
> **- Jackson Kiddard**

You're not one to back down to a challenge, *are you?*

Good, *neither am I.*

The content I provide at BarrelRacingTips.com focuses primarily on the work we do with our horses as it pertains to the pattern and competition. But truth be told, what happens there, is based on what happens *within us first.*

I believe it's time for barrel racers to stop trying to fix problems with their horses by only masking the symptoms. My books and the articles and videos I develop help barrel racers discover the *real reasons* for their challenges, *the truth* about where issues stem from so they can be addressed **at the source** for permanent, lasting, positive results.

My philosophy is the same for this guide. There is a direct connection between our inner and outer reality.

I'll be sharing some techniques for boosting your confidence; don't get me wrong, they are very effective, but remember – they are techniques. Techniques alone will only get you so far if you don't also make a very deep, internal, foundational shift.

I'd like to help you do that, too.

When I reflect back on the personal journey I have traveled, from the point where I started to the person I am today, I can't help but still get a little emotional (so much for being a "tough" barrel racer). The emotion isn't so much due to the lingering pain of the past as it is the joy I feel in the present.

I've spent many years on an intense path of not just growth in horsemanship, but also personal development. When I think about the ways of being that I developed to break free of the pain and dysfunction of my younger years, it was very much "barrel racer style." I didn't know any better at the time, and to be honest, I was desperate. It seemed my only option, but at the core it was fear based.

I simply saw no choice but to become so driven, so aggressive, such an overachiever, that there would be *no chance* that I couldn't do something positive with my life; no chance I could fail. I felt as though I *had to* succeed, as if my life depended on it, and honestly it did.

It *seemed to work*, for a while.

The problem was that my drive was based on *fear of what I didn't want.* And although it seemed effective at the time, it's not the WAY I go about living my life now that I know better.

"Succeeding or else" isn't a healthy, balanced way to think, live and sustain long term. I've by no means "arrived" (we never actually do), but if I can start where I did in life, and develop the foundation of confidence in myself that I have now, *then I know you can too.*

I realized a few years ago that I had a tendency to not take something I learn real seriously until I hear basically the same thing from several different sources. For example, it was only after hearing about six NFR barrel racers stress "the perfect circle," that I REALLY decided that I better pay closer attention to the quality of my circles.

You can read and then put off what I'm sharing here until you suffer some more, or eventually hear something similar five more times over the course of years from other sources. It's my hope though, that what I share will resonate with you in a way that inspires you to implement change now and benefit forever.

I spent a lot of money and time, years in fact, purposely researching, studying, learning and growing. I experienced firsthand the pain limited thinking causes and then dramatic relief as I discovered a path to peace, freedom and confidence. I've sorted through the information, and as I have done in *Secrets to Barrel Racing Success,* am condensing only that which I've found to be most effective into this guide.

The greatest gift you can give me in return, to yourself and especially to the world, is to absorb what you read here, apply it, and put it to good use.

When I mention where I started from, it might bring up memories for you of what you also *didn't get* as a kid (love, praise, support, encouragement, etc.), or ideas about *why* you experience self-doubt. I've spent a lot of time exploring and making sense of my past, but I'll be honest – it's not really that important.

You don't *have to* completely understand why, when or how you developed the beliefs you have. Doing so may be interesting, and may even be somewhat helpful, but it's not necessary. When you spend too much time sorting through the past, and trying to understand it, it can detract from your future and certainly take you out of the present moment.

We're not held back by the love we didn't receive in the past, but by the love we're not extending to ourselves *in the present.* Consider leaving the past where it is, and instead know that all the confidence you desire only requires that you make *a choice* here and now.

> *"I discovered that when I believed my thoughts,*
> *I suffered, but that when I didn't believe them,*
> *I didn't suffer, and that this is true for every human*
> *being. Freedom is as simple as that. I found that*
> *suffering is optional. I found a joy within me that*
> *has never disappeared, not for a single moment.*
> *That joy is in everyone, always."*
> **- Byron Katie**

Let me tell you, I had a hard time with this for a long while. I spent a lot of time riding with a dear friend and mentor who had a grasp on this concept long before I did. I'd often spout out reasons why I struggled with this or that in a run, why my horses did this or that. I was always analyzing and wanting to figure out WHY things weren't going the way I wanted.

What a waste of time! All that analyzing was only getting in my way.

Terrible things *can and do* happen in life, and it's' important to fully feel and process our emotions, but life challenges can only damage our confidence and change the way we think and act *if we let them.*

My friend used to say "It doesn't matter, it doesn't matter!"

Pfffttt!? How annoying! *Easy for HER to say,* I used to think... *SHE doesn't have the past experiences that make things so hard for ME.*

Well, that belief was my problem – I felt this need to figure out WHY certain things were "hard for me." They *were hard*, because I believed they were. I had tunnel vision directed toward what was so hard. I didn't see it at the time, but by doing so, I was creating excuses, I was applying limitations.

When I released my attachment and just chose a different path and firmly decided to change my hand position in a turn or trust my horse at the first barrel, *I just did it.* NO MORE excuses about WHY I couldn't, or *why* it was hard. Lasting change can REALLY happen *that fast,* you just have to make a choice - *it's that simple.*

Are YOU ready to make the rest of your life, the best of your life?

When I reflect on everything I've been through and the insights I've gained, I realize that there's no way I could *not* share what I've learned to help others.

Enjoy "The Confident Barrel Racer," I hope it makes a positive difference in your life.

With Gratitude,

Heather Smith

> *The principle of competing is against yourself. It's about self-improvement, about being better than you were the day before.*

– Steve Young

THE CHALLENGE OF COMPETITION

Before we begin, you should know about a certain challenge we commonly bump up against as barrel racers (which of course, I'll help you overcome).

To start, I'd venture to say that anyone who is a competitor of any kind, will especially struggle with confidence - more so than someone who does not compete.

WHY?

Because competition creates a winner and a loser. If you were consistently clocking in the 1D and then for three runs in a row weren't even in the 4D, you might start thinking, *"I'm such a loser!"* You might even start thinking that after one less than stellar run. Competition creates an environment that celebrates winning, and well, there are no saddles, gigantic checks, and photo shoots for anyone who doesn't clock well enough to place.

Through the act of declaring a winner, an underlying message is created saying "this person IS good, and these people are NOT." Competition - as fun, and challenging, and wonderful as it is, does have its downside. Competition can join like-minded people together, but in a sense, it also creates a dramatic separation. If even on a subconscious level, it assigns labels based on performance. So of course it's common when we win or perform well, to feel good, to feel like we are enough, and when we don't win or perform well, we feel the opposite. This is quite a conundrum, because we can't possibly win them all!

As I've mentioned, barrel racers seem to have an unspoken image to uphold. For young people especially, it seems like it's cool to be "tough." It's cool to "kick ass." There's this drive to receive some kind of ego boost (which comes when we do well in competition) that says to our subconscious mind "I'm better than the rest." As barrel racers, we are often conditioned to develop a tom-boyish, overly masculine and aggressive way of fighting for what we want.

The nature of competition creates separation, it creates judgment, it puts a wedge between "good enough" and "not good enough," and make no mistake, this presents a challenge when it comes to our confidence.

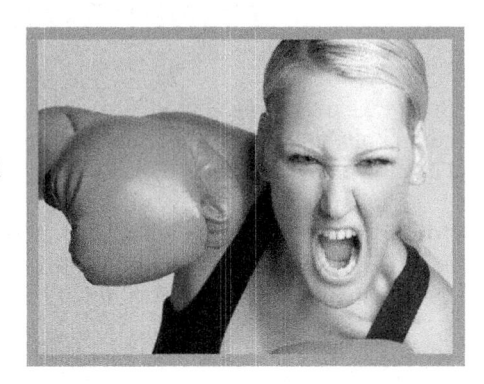

I realize that barrel racing wouldn't be nearly as exciting if we all held hands by the horse trailer to sing "Kum ba yah" and there were equal prizes and money given to every participant, and of course, that's not what I'm suggesting.

However, it's helpful to realize that the nature of competition can do a number to our confidence if we're not careful. Competition can breed non-acceptance.

Just by being part of barrel racing, or any competitive environment, we're also becoming more susceptible to developing less acceptance and more judgment toward others, and therefore ourselves as well. Competing can contribute to a tendency to question our worth.

To stand out in any arena of life means you can't hide from the thoughts and opinions of others, which requires a very firm inner foundation. Being involved in competition can make developing and maintaining confidence challenging, but again, my goal is to help barrel racers *overcome challenges,* and this guide will help you overcome *this one,* specifically.

Basically, just like speed emphasizes the holes in our horse's development, competing emphasizes the holes in our emotional foundation. If you didn't put yourself out there, you might not even know they exist. If we're not consistently stretching ourselves, it's easy to settle into the comfort that lulls us into believing there's no need for any inner work.

When our weak spots our brought to our attention and made obvious, we have a special opportunity to grow and strengthen this inner foundation, which will benefit us in all areas of life.

Perhaps having an aggressive "do or die" mentality has proven to be effective for creating results in your barrel racing. Maybe it seems like fear of losing has helped you win.

In reality, a "win or else" approach puts unnecessary, unhealthy and unproductive pressure on ourselves and our horses. This is essentially a way we protect ourselves, like carrying a big, heavy shield that keeps us weighed down and stuck. It may seem to prevent us from losing but it's actually holding us back from winning.

I know with certainty that if your confidence is sourced *entirely* from the outside, or if your drive to win is based on fear of what you *don't want* (to lose), then you're not only putting a limit on your success, but missing out on the joy of barrel racing, and life.

It's time to put down the shield.

> *All the concepts about stepping out of your comfort zone mean nothing until you decide that your essential purpose, vision and goals are more important than your self-imposed limitations.*

– Robert White

ARE YOU READY?

On the following pages I'll be sharing more about where I feel true confidence is sourced from. I hope you're inspired and excited to learn about how it's possible to develop a deep, lasting sense of confidence that never wavers when you blast down the alley. Before I go any further though, I need to be absolutely sure.

Now I don't consider myself a confrontational person. With occasional bursts of extroversion, I'm really an introvert who would rather avoid conflict whenever possible, but right now is a critical point. I have to go outside my comfort zone here.

If I knew you wouldn't report me to the authorities, with deep, grounded and fierce love, I'd firmly grab both your arms and pull you aside at a barrel race. I'd look into your eyes and with all seriousness and powerful emotion, I would ask you...

> *"Did you know that this life is a gift, and you were only given one? Do you realize that allowing negative thoughts and feelings of self-doubt effect you is like voluntarily locking yourself in jail? That the only thing holding you back from achieving your wildest barrel racing dreams is YOU? Do you know that your outer reality, and how you perceive it, is a reflection of what you have going on within? Do you know how much more joy, peace, and happiness is possible?*
>
> *You were not put on this earth by accident, and so it's time to start becoming more intentional about the joyous expansion you were intended to experience and share. You can't do this alone. You were given certain gifts in this life, but it is up to you to use them. If you let your mind run on "auto-pilot" you are not doing your part, you are not fully appreciating the gift of life you have been given.*
>
> *Are you ready to break free of self-imposed limitations, to step out of imaginary jail and realize your potential? Do you know how quickly your life can turn around when you do?*

That the cycle of negative thinking can stop right this moment and change your life forever?

Are you ready to take the imaginary chains off your horse's legs, and unleash your wildest dreams? Are you ready and willing to make a choice, right here, right NOW, as if your very life depended on it?"

If your answer is *"Yes,"* GOOD, because **IT DOES!**

Marianne Williamson actually gets a similar message across much better than I...

"Our deepest fear is not that we are inadequate. Our deepest fear is that we are powerful beyond measure. It is our light, not our darkness that most frightens us. We ask ourselves, Who am I to be brilliant, gorgeous, talented, fabulous? Actually, who are you not to be? You are a child of God. Your playing small does not serve the world. There is nothing enlightened about shrinking so that other people won't feel insecure around you. We are all meant to shine, as children do. We were born to make manifest the glory of God that is within us. It's not just in some of us; it's in everyone. And as we let our own light shine, we unconsciously give other people permission to do the same. As we are liberated from our own fear, our presence automatically liberates others."

At this point, you may either be in tears, or maybe that crunchy barrel racer exterior hasn't softened a bit, and you think I'm wacko. Either way, it's OK.

Because of my inner foundation of confidence, I can accept that some people might think I'm wacko, and not care one bit. My desire to help others is stronger than my desire to look good and have everyone's approval.

If you're ready to continue, let's get on with it, *shall we?*

> *"Life... it tends to respond to our outlook, to shape itself to meet our expectations."*
> **- Richard M. DeVos**

> **It's not your job to like me - it's mine.**

- Byron Katie

FIERCE LOVE

We all know it takes confidence to WIN, but many barrel racers don't feel confident *until* they win. Ugh! It's like the chicken and the egg.

So how does a person, without a ton of sheer beginner's luck, get from point A to B? My friend, that is where the deep well of confidence comes in, the one with depths that may change slightly, but win or lose, never runs dry.

The first of numerous truths I will share is one that contradicts the underlying message that competition delivers (and seems contradictory in itself), but is true none the less.

That is, that on a deep level *we are all the same.*

We are all created with a specific purpose on this earth that only we can fulfill; to embrace who we uniquely are and OWN it. We are ALL enough, important, and yet each talented (albeit in different ways) with gifts to give the world, our loved ones and horses, that only we can give.

This inner knowing is where our foundational, unshakable confidence stems from. Belief in ourselves and or worth is NOT generated from the outside, it comes from a well deep within.

"You have all you need within you to become the best version of yourself. Anything that inspires you is an outward reflection of the potential within you. Cultivate in your own life, in your own way, the qualities and greatness you see in others and pretty soon you will be living a life that is your personal version of greatness. Your work is to apply yourself every day and don't look back."
- Jackson Kiddard

Of course we can look to others for inspiration, but just because someone is a highly accomplished world champion barrel racer, doesn't make them a better person than you.

We are all valuable just because we exist, not because of what we DO, or our list of accomplishments. It's easy, as barrel racers to get very wrapped up in comparison, or the results we achieve. I'm here to tell you – achievements in the arena do not determine your worth.

If you're waiting to feel content until you check some achievement off your list, or if part of the reason you so desperately pursue your goals is to finally feel like you're enough, you've got it backwards.

We all have dormant potential and it's up to each of us to realize it. Because you were born, because you were created - that fact automatically makes you valuable, not any more so, or less so, than anyone else – *anyone.* You are enough. You are special. You are one of a kind. You are loved. You are, just because YOU ARE!

> *"Self-confidence means to truly love ourselves*
> *at the deepest level. This is the definition of*
> *self-confidence - what confidence means."*
> – Bruce Eisner

So you might wonder - "How can I remember this, and *still* be part of a competitive world, and still 'run with the wolves' and even lead the pack (all the way to the pay window)?"

Loving and accepting yourself and others while remaining fiercely aggressive in competition IS possible, but doing so involves developing a deep, internal foundation, and may also require new awareness and perspectives. As I go on to describe below, it's *not* something I believe you can do alone.

No Matter What

What if your horse rocketed around the second barrel so hard that you lost your balanced and tumbled off to the ground? What if your horse was blasting home from the third barrel and suddenly exploded into a bucking fit?

Things DO happen in life that either chip away or take big chunks out of our confidence. When things like this happen, our subconscious minds go to work in sort of an overprotective effort to make sure that history doesn't repeat itself. We think, "I hope he doesn't buck," "I hope I don't screw up and look bad." Again, these thoughts are deep and instinctual, because we want to stay safe, have approval, be liked by others, and accepted as part of the caveman tribe.

But wait a minute... *we're not cavemen anymore!*

Truth be told, it's high time we developed ways of thinking that serve us better. Again, there are times that the thoughts that run through our mind are there for good reason – they actually DO help us survive and stay safe, and should NOT always be completely ignored. However, the majority of these thoughts are completely irrational. Your survival doesn't depend on the crowd's approval. As you may have found, having such a desire does more harm than good, especially when your mind drifts to your desired outcome, or to what other people might think, and takes your precious focus away from where it should be.

Worrying incessantly over things that haven't actually happened, is a lot like praying for what you don't want. The more you think about what you don't want – the more likely it is you'll get it!

> *"Peace. It does not mean to be in a place where there is no trouble, noise, or hard work. It means to be in the midst of those things and still be calm in your heart."*
> - **Lady Gaga**

When we worry and allow our minds to spin in a way that doesn't feel good, the *not so pleasant* emotions we experience are the body's reaction to the mind. Essentially our thoughts become emotions and feelings, which then reflect back to us in the form of our results, environment, relationships and outer reality.

I'm not saying there aren't things that make life challenging, but that the majority of the difficulty we experience comes from the inside, it comes from our perception of what happens. It's our mind that decides *for us* what is "good vs. bad." When our mind is running on autopilot, we're essentially giving our power away and taking on a helpless, victim role - and we all know THAT's not *"barrel racer style!"*

> *"Although I may not be able to prevent the worst from happening, I am responsible for my attitude toward the inevitable misfortunes that darken life. Bad things do happen; how I respond to them defines my character and the quality of my life. I can choose to sit in perpetual sadness, immobilized by the gravity of my loss, or I can choose to rise from the pain and treasure the most precious gift I have - life itself."*
> **- Walter Anderson**

When you pull into the parking lot at a rodeo does your stomach start to turn as you worry about finding a place to park, or getting to the entry office in time, or do you think *"This is going to be the most fun EVER"?*

It's essential that we have more control over how we feel. If you change the way you think, it changes the way you feel, which changes the way you act, what you do and ultimately your whole world.

So often we allow what happens on the outside determine how we feel on the inside. When we do, it's as if we're on a constant emotional roller coaster.

What if it could be different?

What if you had a foundational, baseline level of confidence that just plain didn't change – no matter what!? What if your confidence was so strong, that it just didn't matter what happened in the arena or out? What if it didn't matter whether you felt especially prepared, or how your performance went, or what your friends or family said or thought, what your time was, or how you placed. What if you were just a living, breathing, walking ball of confidence regardless of your circumstances!? I don't mean a superficial, or false, ego-inflated confidence, but grateful, radiating, humble confidence. What if you were overflowing with so much of it, that others around you couldn't help but feel confident too, just by being in your presence?

> *"There is only one you for all time. Fearlessly be yourself."*
> - **Anthony Rapp**

We CAN achieve this foundational level of confidence that never wavers, but there's only one way to do it, that I've discovered...

> *...that is through the relationship with your self, and with your source.*

If you have love in your life it can make up for a great many things you lack. If you don't have it, no matter what else there is, it's not enough.

- Ann Landers

SOURCE & SELF

Wikipedia's definition of **con·fi·dence** is...

> *"The feeling or belief that one can rely on someone or something; firm trust... the state of feeling certain about the truth of something."*

Although we must have more influence over our thoughts, developing confidence is definitely NOT something we do by ourselves, it's done in partnership. Just as the definition above describes, confidence is a belief or feeling that we *"can rely on someone or something; firm trust... feeling certain about the truth."*

Yet previously I shared a definition of self-confidence describing it as *"loving ourselves at the deepest level."* What I perceive as **confidence** is a *beautiful merging* of these two definitions.

In the past I've been fortunate to spend time riding one on one with some incredible horsemen. These amazing people were my respected mentors and also became my friends. There was a problem that would come up for me when we'd ride together, though. They would be talking and sharing some ideas about what I should try doing differently, all in a genuine effort to help me, and as I was trying so hard to implement their suggestions, the tears would start welling up. I often had a hard time holding them back. I didn't completely understand what was happening at the time.

"Speak about yourself in positive and constructive terms only. Never sell yourself short."
- Brian Tracy

What I eventually realized, was that the voice of my (terribly cruel) inner critic would get *so loud* (in that environment especially), that I would actually twist around what my mentors were saying and interpret it as something very negative.

Essentially my inner critic was beating me up mentally to such a degree that tears started flowing due to the hurtful emotions I experienced.

They might have said "try lifting your hand and using it more like this..." and I would translate it into "You're so worthless, you're never going to get it!"

Can you see how irrational that was, how far from reality the things my mind came up with were?

Based on my sniffles and watery eyes, it was all *very real* to me at the time. I see now that those negative voices – they were all *complete and utter lies.*

The things your inner critic says are too.

Even though I had read tons of personal development books, about ten years ago I stumbled across one that changed my life forever.

It's titled "Do You Think I'm Beautiful" by **Angela Thomas**, and I highly recommend it (I've also suggested several other resources at the conclusion of this book).

It seems obvious now looking back, why I didn't have much confidence up to that point. Until I read that book, I didn't have a clue about where this foundation of confidence came from.

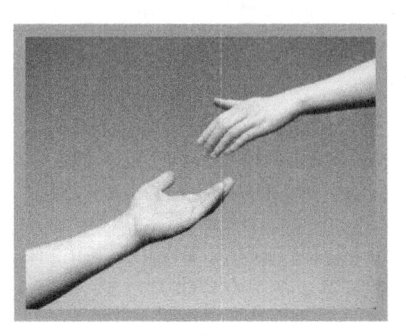

What I learned during that time, was that I wasn't alone; that the weight of the world was not on my shoulders. I realized that I didn't need to be in control and worry about everything myself.

What a stress reliever!

I had finally found that *"someone or something"* that we have to trust in order to feel confidence! For the first time, I really started learning all about this "special someone" who was crazy in love with me, ME!

I could hardly believe it at first, but by that point, I was more than ready for **the truth**. I had suffered enough. I cried tears of joy and relief for literally weeks. Until that point, I hadn't really been aware of and understood the love that existed for me. Even though I explain this love as coming from a source outside of myself, it's actually so deep and strong that it lives and works *in and through me* every day, and in every way.

When this happened, for the first time my inner critic shut up. Not because I kicked her ass, but because I LOVED HER TO DEATH.

Now the "ghost of inner critics past" still shows up now and then.   Quieting her back down is often a matter of remembering to nurture the relationship with that "someone or something," and at the same time nurturing the relationship with myself.

> *"We don't need self-confidence, We need God-confidence."*
> - Joyce Meyer

I personally call that special someone God. I firmly believe that having a strong relationship with a power greater than yourself - one that you know has your best interest in mind, that you can surrender your problems and worries to, that you can ask for help, confide in, that you can trust, and that loves you more than you can even begin to imagine, IS where that true, foundational inner well of confidence is sourced from – THE SOURCE, that which created you. All those years ago, I found the source of **confidence.** Today, I wouldn't be doing a service to anyone if I didn't share it.

Without this understanding and belief, I would have never found true peace, happiness and confidence. Just like my horsemanship, I'm on a continuous journey of developing my relationship to "source and self," and nurturing the connection between the two as I go.

Sometimes we just need a reminder of how important these relationships are, which is OK, because it's easy to forget. I can't really share any truth with you that you don't already know, but I'm happy to remind you of what you may have forgotten.

Over the course of many years now, I've been getting better at caring for myself more like God would care for me – that's with LOTS of love.

I realized that He would *never* approve of the horribly cruel name-calling in my head.

Our creator has big plans for me, AND YOU, which is why it's important that we take *great care of ourselves* so that we can serve our purpose to the best of our ability. This isn't just about taking care of our physical health, but our mental and  emotional health, by purposely choosing uplifting thoughts. We've all abused ourselves in some way, either mentally, physically, emotionally, or all three. When you adopt this perspective, treating yourself kindly and developing practices that build, rather than tear down confidence, becomes so much easier.

For example, it wasn't until I trusted God with the success of my career that I could surrender my workaholic tendencies enough to allow myself eight hours of sleep a night. Turns out I can serve the world and accomplish much greater things from a place of fullness.

If you're on an airplane that might crash, you'll only be able to help other people with their oxygen mask if you put yours on first. Great self-care isn't about being selfish or narcissistic. Only when we show *ourselves* the love that exists for us, can we show up fully in life and share it with others, like our children, family, spouses, and our horses.

> *"Trust in the LORD and do good;*
> *Dwell in the land and enjoy safe pasture.*
> *Take delight in the LORD,*
> *And he will give you the desires of your heart."*
> - **Psalm 37:3-4**

Relationships with others start with the one you have with yourself, and the relationship you have with yourself has everything to do with your relationship to **source.**

As these relationships deepen, it's as if they merge in a way. It's as if love is no longer something you do, but something you become. You embody love as a way of being, and as a result, it radiates through you and becomes your new "default setting." Powerful love exists *in us* and works *through us* in miraculous ways, giving us the capacity to choose love in all situations.

If I hadn't come to this realization, I would not be writing these words right now.

I've helped people in varying ways in the past, but it wasn't until my relationship with "self and source" was cultivated to a deeper level, that I had an overwhelming desire to share my lessons and help others on a much larger scale.

Honestly, in the past I found it hard to be genuinely happy for other people's success,

> *"Right now, and in every now-moment, you are either closing or opening. You are either stressfully waiting for something - more money, security, affection - or you are living from your deep heart, opening as the entire moment, and giving what you most deeply desire to give, without waiting."*
> - **David Deida**

and I didn't give out too many compliments. It's no wonder, because I was really empty on the inside. I didn't have any good stuff to spare.

Because of the confidence I feel today, I am more outgoing than I ever have been. I have a joy and happiness within that can't NOT be shared.

Because I understand and believe in the love that exists for me, and do my best to love myself and others in the same way, I'm overflowing with confidence. Negativity and self-doubt simply can't co-exist with this deep love.

My baseline confidence level is not dependent on the outside, so it stays firm regardless of my circumstances. I have a foundational sense of peace and contentedness that doesn't waver. The voice of my inner critic no longer pipes up when I trot down the alley. I don't slip into a negative downward mental and emotional spiral when my horse gets hurt or my husband gets laid off.

Sometimes I temporarily forget about these truths, but I quickly remember to spend time nurturing that relationship of trust, where I'm reminded that I can tackle anything that comes my way with CONFIDENCE. This one major understanding and belief can change everything, forever, when it comes to the confidence we feel. If these ideas are new to you, I hope you'll consider them. If you're familiar with the relationships to *source and self* I write of, I hope you'll be reminded to care for and strengthen them.

As we go forward, remember that although the tools and techniques provided throughout this guide are extremely valuable and effective, that they are just techniques. Without a foundational belief in "someone or something" you can trust, that created you and loves you more than you can imagine, I feel as though the path to finding true confidence will be a challenging one.

> *Fear of failure and fear of the unknown are always defeated by faith. Having faith in yourself, in the process of change, and in the new direction that change sets will reveal your own inner core of steel.*

- Georgette Mosbacher

FOUR STEPS TO CONFIDENCE

Awareness, Reflection, Change, Integration

For barrel racers, symptoms of low confidence may show up as difficulty focusing before and during a run, and/or feelings of overwhelming nervousness. If we dissect this tendency to spin mentally or experience anxiety, we usually find that the culprit is the negative self-talk I've referred to previously.

As I have mentioned, I believe we co-create our life in partnership with He who created us. However, if we prayed all day, every day but never got off the couch, where would that get us? If you wanted to "attract" a new horse into your life, but didn't take any action, such as saving money or searching the classified ads, it's not very likely that your intention will become reality.

We've been given a body and a mind, but it's up to us to use them. It's important to be open to divine guidance and have a foundational relationship built on love and trust. We're not alone in this. However, as in any relationship, both ends need to do their part. In this case, the other part *has already been done.* So we need to take the physical and mental abilities given to us and put them into action.

For the first 20 years of my life, the negative chatter in my mind was out of control, but for the most part, I didn't even realize it. It wasn't until I started becoming driven to accomplish big things in the arena that I started to take note of the little things that were getting in my way. I realized that my thoughts were actually a huge obstacle standing in the way of my success.

The first step toward permanent change was **AWARENESS.**

Maybe your inner critic has never beat you to tears, but there might be quite a bit of "not so positive" talk going on upstairs that you don't even realize. The first step toward eradicating it, is paying closer attention.

Does your inner critic pipe up when you ride with other people? In those moments before a run? When performing in front of a big crowd, when the energy is high or when the announcer and music is especially loud? After a run that didn't go as well as you hoped? Does the negative self-talk occur during or after you've spent time with a certain person? When you actually take time to relax? Do you tend to negatively critique or judge others? Identify these thinking errors, which can actually include negative self-talk, expectations, labels, judgment, comparison, generalizations, irrational beliefs, etc.

> *"See if you can catch yourself complaining in either speech or thought, about a situation you find yourself in, what other people do or say, your surroundings, your life situation, even the weather. To complain is always non-acceptance of what is. It invariably carries an unconscious negative charge. When you complain, you make yourself a victim. Leave the situation or accept it. All else is madness."*
> **- Eckhart Tolle**

The exact words or visuals that occur in our minds vary from person to person, but a similar thread runs through it all, a message saying – "You're not enough." As I've explained, this statement is completely false.

Of course, it's great to be working toward your barrel racing goals or improving your *life situation*, but your LIFE is perfect, YOU are perfect – just exactly as you are. There's nothing you can do or not do to change your worth as a human being. You are MORE THAN ENOUGH, just because you EXIST.

Remember, without awareness, there can be no change. Don't allow new found awareness to become an excuse to be even harder on yourself. The fact that you're noticing your thinking errors is a reason to celebrate!

A second step toward reforming the voice of your inner critic is **REFLECTION.**

Once you've become more aware of the soundtrack or mental movies in your mind and the circumstances in which they tend to occur, simply sit back and take on the role of observer.

Do you notice any particular patterns? Imagine you're sitting in the rafters, looking down on yourself from up above and listening in to the conversations that are taking place in your mind. Seeing yourself like this, and watching as an outsider can be especially eye-opening. This helps you recognize self-talk in a disassociated way. When you do, you're not as personally immersed in it, and less likely to believe it. It can wake you up to the fact that the voices aren't accurate, that what your inner critic is saying isn't true! You might even begin to laugh at the craziness of it all!

Pffffttt! How could you believe those things!?

Reflection is about disconnecting yourself from the negative voice in your own mind. It's not you, and it's *not* the truth. You are not your mind. Just this realization alone can relieve us of so much pain. It has the power to remove blocks standing in the way of the barrel racing success you've always wanted.

> *"Promise me you'll always remember:*
> *You're braver than you believe,*
> *and stronger than you seem,*
> *and smarter than you think."*
> **- Christopher Robin**

Once we've reflected on our patterns from a new angle, it's time to **CHANGE** in the moment.

When my husband was laid off from his job a couple years ago, he was somewhat of a "Negative Ned" for a few days. I didn't get on his case too harshly, but I did casually point out the errors in his thinking. I'd say, "Ya know Craig, another way to think about it would be like this, and this...", etc.

Then one weekend morning not long after that I was up early and he came trudging into the kitchen, looking a little disheveled as everyone does only minutes from waking. I decided to give him some good natured grief, because he had that same cranky look on his face that he'd been wearing for days. I immediately started acting like a four year old having a temper tantrum, and teasingly asked, *"Let me guess, you HATE waking up!?"* We had a laugh and I reminded him what the alternative could be – *NOT WAKING UP!*

On a recent trip we ate at a restaurant called the "Hog's Breath Saloon," and I noticed a sign on the wall that read "Hog's breath is better than no breath!"

How true! When you find yourself complaining or not feeling so good about something, cold weather for example, remind yourself, *"Cold air is better than NO air!"*

> *"You must take personal responsibility. You cannot change the circumstances, the seasons, or the wind, but you can change yourself. That is something you have charge of. You don't have charge of the constellations, but you do have charge of whether you read, develop new skills, and take new classes."*
> **- Jim Rohn**

As your awareness grows, you'll become better at catching yourself thinking about anything negative. When you do, it's time to turn it around into something positive.

It's helpful to keep in mind that everything around you is subjective to a variety of perceptions. Characteristics that you love in a barrel horse, someone else might hate. You might enjoy rainy days, I prefer the sunshine! Every situation can feel how you want it to feel, based on how you think about it. Nothing is really good or bad – it's our thoughts and feelings that make them that way. It doesn't serve you to assume the worst. If you're going to be making up stories in your head, by all means it would serve you better to tell ones that feel good!

If your mind starts to tell a story that doesn't feel good, take your power back. If you find yourself down in the dumps, retrace your steps. You're not a helpless victim of your mind. You have a choice when it comes to how you interpret what happens in life and what you want to see, feel, experience and be.

Whenever you find yourself focusing on anything negative, STOP and look hard for the positive in your situation. There is ALWAYS something - look until you find it, then find more. Even in what seem like the worst possible circumstances, there will always be silver linings, IF you are willing to choose a different perspective.

Start by telling a better-feeling story about everything you encounter. When you find yourself in a funk, you might even repeat a mantra in your mind, *"Find a better-feeling thought, find a better-feeling thought, find a better-feeling thought."*

Do whatever it takes to change your mind, which might be some inspirational reading, positive music, an uplifting YouTube video, a phone call to a friend, a walk in nature - whatever makes you feel good!

Maybe your horse gets seriously injured, like mine did a while back. Of course I was upset, but instantly I started to look for the blessing in disguise. I thought that maybe there were lessons for me to teach and learn with another horse for the time being. Maybe the months that followed were to be better spent working on my new book?

As you become more skilled at switching gears in your mind, you'll be able to get back on track and head in a positive direction even more quickly. You'll recover from the disappointment you feel after a bad run in a few minutes vs. a few days. You'll see setbacks as temporary, rather than permanent or something that defines you as a person. You'll release attachment to outcomes and believe that each moment in life is perfect, even if something doesn't turn out like you hoped. You'll be more likely to recognize and appreciate the lesson and gift in any adversity.

The more time you spend in a mental state of positivity and appreciation, the more happiness and reasons to be grateful you'll find in your life. You'll feel happy and confident "for no reason."

> A helpful technique for change in the moment involves purposefully thinking of something that brings you a lot of happiness. Picture whatever that is in your mind so the image is vivid and bright. Then imagine the feelings you experience are actually spinning in your body. Feel the positive emotions swirling around and allow the image to cover the screen of your mind and become very lifelike. Now picture whatever it is you feel bad about. Maybe you see it as a small black and white picture in the corner of your mind. Instead, bring it up in place of the positive image. Keep spinning that same positive feeling and join it with whatever you weren't feeling so good about. Associate the feelings you experienced with the first image and apply them to the second, which is now front and center in your mind - very bright, warm and positive.

"Lorie darlin,' life in San Francisco, you see, is still just life. If you want any one thing too badly, it's likely to turn out to be a disappointment. The only healthy way to live life is to learn to like all the little everyday things, like a sip of good whiskey in the evening, a soft bed, a glass of buttermilk, or a feisty gentleman like myself."
– Augustus McCrae, Lonesome Dove

The fourth stage of change is **INTEGRATION**, when your new positive habits have become second nature.

Like I've mentioned, it's not very realistic to think that if we're "doin' it right," that we'll never have another negative thought.

Even the highest achieving people in the world have moments of doubt and insecurity. If we didn't, it would mean we were never daring new things and going outside our comfort zones.

In addition, there's nothing wrong with fully feeling pain, sadness, anger, grief and other emotions when they come up, in fact you should. The trouble occurs when we allow feelings and emotions to control us or take over in inappropriate and unhealthy ways that don't actually serve us in the long run.

> *"What you make of your life is up to you. You have all the tools and resources you need. Your answers lie inside of you."*
> **- Denis Waitley**

Achieving integration means that you have more positive "default" thinking than negative. You can allow your mind to drift on autopilot and when it does, you're more likely to think uplifting thoughts, about what you're grateful for, and what you want vs. what you don't want, and what you love instead of what you fear. You spend more time enjoying the peace of the present moment compared to regretting the past or having anxiety about the future.

We don't have to allow the same negative tapes to play over and over and continuously chip away at our confidence. We can catch these thoughts in the act and intentionally choose new ones. We have a choice. We are not a bundle of conditioned reflexes. Again, I believe we create our lives in partnership with He who created us. We may not have control of everything that happens in life, but we DO have control over how we feel about it.

So stay on your toes, nurture the relationship to self & source and practice developing your awareness and ability to debunk the lies.

If we are to experience true confidence, I believe we must take responsibility for our part. You CAN change your thoughts and establish new set points. When you do, you'll be amazed how quickly your barrel racing success and the dreams planted in your heart become reality.

> *I can feel guilty about the past, apprehensive about the future, but only in the present can I act. The ability to be in the present moment is a major component of mental wellness.*

- Abraham Maslow

GET PRESENT

You're probably beginning to see that the mind is an amazing tool – IF used correctly. Unfortunately, most of us don't use our mind at all, it uses us! We all too often lack awareness, and because so many are in the same boat – it's become the norm.

I'm not up for being "the norm" however, and I know you aren't either. So I'm excited to take you to a special place where the mental activity that lowers our confidence CANNOT exist!

That is, *in the moment.*

When it comes to understanding what "being in the present moment" is and *how* to get there, we can learn all about it best from animals and nature.

If my gelding Pistol asked the cactus *"Hey man, do you know what time it is?"* The cactus might reply, *"Whataya mean? The time is NOW, what else is there!?"* The only way Pistol could ever get wind of what "time" was, would be from ME!

After all, if he were to read my thoughts, they might sound like this…

"Only 30 minutes to ride…work on forward quality movement and full-body bend… finish article this afternoon, run to town, post office, bank, feed store, call for exhibitions and stalls, what's for lunch tomorrow, I'm hungry…"

"To do two things at once is to do neither."
- Publilius Syrus

When it comes to learning how to be more present, animals are the best teachers. They live moment to moment without schedules and goals. When they feel joy, they let 'er rip and jump and leap in the air! When they get irritated they may also leap in the air, or squeal, pin their ears, kick, but then they get over it and move on.   In their natural environment with other horses, they feel fully in the moment, without hesitation or repression.

Small children can teach us many of the same lessons, because they haven't yet forgotten how to be in the moment, as adults have.

Can YOU be in the moment and feel pure joy? Or does it have to be sunny, or do you have to have a pumpkin spice latte to enjoy the moment? Can you enjoy the present organically without any sprinkles on top? Do you have so much on your plate that being in the moment seems impossible?

Have perceptions of your life being a burden or struggle covered up the pure joy of the moment? The sunshine and a good latte can bring you pleasure, which is great, but joy can be yours in *every moment.*

If there isn't joy, ease or lightness in what you're doing, you may just need to change HOW. Experiment with giving your fullest attention to whatever the moment presents, rather than a result you want to achieve.

My Australian Shepherd, Tess reminds me to celebrate the joy in each moment. When I'm putting my boots on and my hair back to do chores she starts bounding around my feet. Even though she's a canine senior citizen these days, she twists and bounces in the air with excitement that cannot be contained.

SHE KNOWS, if I am putting boots on, we just MUST be going on a GREAT ADVENTURE!

She's right ya know!

She reminds me that, YES, *doing chores* CAN be a grand adventure IF I think of it that way!

So on my way to feed, I stop as I walk out the door and let the warm Texas air give me a hug.   As I'm picking horse manure with all my focused attention, I'm reminded of how grateful I am to have the opportunity to own and learn from such beautiful animals. I run my hands over Pistol's dark, shiny chestnut coat. I pause and just listen and watch him eat while I notice the subtle contrast in the shades of lighter brown hair on his face and the kind, softness of his eyes.

In the midst of peaceful pause I'm reminded of how much I love and appreciate him. As I finish chores, I see Tess waiting for me at the gate. I give her the release command, she races to me and then we both bounce for the sheer joy of it – yep, doing chores IS a *great adventure!*

All because of the thoughts I choose in the present moment!

Doing vs. Being

In a world that places a very high value on *doing* and *accomplishing,* being present in the moment, and its benefits, are not something that is fully understood or appreciated. Because we are human *beings,* not human *doings,* it's certainly worthwhile to learn more about what it means to "be here now."

Humans get very wrapped up in the concept of "time." So many of us live in a constant mental spin of preparation for the future. We're really anxious for it because on a deep level, we're somehow convinced that it will be better than the past or the present.  The down side to this is that we risk missing the moments as they pass.

If you become too excessively focused on a future goal, perhaps in an effort to find happiness, fulfillment, or feel complete, the *now* is no longer honored. It just becomes a stepping stone to the future, with no value.

When this happens, you're inviting the negative self-talk to move into your mental space and limiting the level of peace, happiness and confidence you feel. When you spend too much time thinking about what "might be" you lose appreciation for what IS.

Truthfully, though, there has never been a time that is *not now*, and there never will be. When you feel nervous, and are full of anxiety, worry and "what ifs" about the future, that's where your mind has wondered. In the "now," these thoughts lose their negative charge.

Think of it like having a mental screen saver. When you go "idle" those negative thoughts pop up, but when you're fully engaged in whatever you're doing, they disappear. It's OK to feel sadness, regret, anxiety, fear or worry at times, but feel those emotions fully as well, and then move on. When you remain in the present moment and process emotions completely, they no longer hold power to drain your confidence.

Experiencing recurrent negative thoughts, feeling stress of any kind, or even complaining, are all forms of resistance. It's non-acceptance of what IS. It carries negativity that actually plays a part in creating your future. When we're in the moment, we release attachment to things our mind judges as "good or bad" and can finally get off the emotional roller coaster.

> *"Nothing is perfect if judgment is present.*
> *Everything is perfect when you let go –*
> *this is how you see with the eyes of love."*
> **- Jackson Kiddard**

High speed, extreme sports like barrel racing can force us into the "now," which is one reason why so many people enjoy these activities. It's a momentous escape from our overly active minds. Often times, barrel racers can't even escape their minds for the 14-18 seconds that it may take to run the barrel pattern. Our minds constant chatter still gets in our way – and slows us down! Learning how to be present in the moment can change that.

When you're fully aware and present in the moment, you are focusing only on the task at hand. You put all your attention on the task before you, and do so with quality, care and love. When it's time to make a run - it's you, your horse, the clock and nothing else. When you're in the present moment as you're blasting down the alley, there is no way you can get psyched out, because being present quiets the mental chatter and allows you to focus on what you need to do – when you're in the moment, you can't NOT ride your very best.

In this mental place, you're not thinking about how much money is at stake, if your horse will refuse the gate, how many people are watching, whether you'll look good or not. You are focused in like a laser ONLY on what you are there to do in every single fraction of a second in that run.

Do your thought patterns interfere with your NOW? Is your life so full that you feel forced to multi-task mentally in order to keep all your plates in the air? Are you always hoping to cross some kind of (ever-moving) finish line? Anything worth doing is worth doing ALL THE WAY, not half way. Being overly goal oriented however, can take the joy out of the now. Right now, you are perfect, and you are *enough.*

This state of simply BEING rather than doing is very much connected with the deep relationships I wrote of earlier on. Eventually the edges of separation fade and life becomes more about who you are vs. what you do – a human being, not a human doing.

Be Here Now

There's nothing wrong with setting goals or planning for the future, but when you do, do it fully. Everything you do, do it with your full attention. Anything *worth doing,* deserves it! Multi-tasking is completely overrated. Your horses, your family, your work, etc. all deserve your full attention.

If you feel unable to give your best, it may be a sign that you need to simplify and prioritize your life based on what is most important. When you're fully immersed in something, you'll be amazed at the results that the quality of your focus produces (without ever having to think about it)! It's a natural byproduct of being in the moment.

When you're in this state of being, how can you not succeed?

A helpful tip for sinking into the moment, is simply noticing silence. Dr. Wayne Dyer said that the space between the notes makes the music and the space between the bars holds the tiger. Be aware of the gaps - put your attention on them. Paying attention to outer silence helps the mind quiet and create the kind of inner silence that allows us to fully focus on the task before us.

Another method for dropping into the NOW, is to actually FEEL your inner body. Get quiet and feel the sensations of the energy moving in your body, feel the rhythm of your pulse beating. Keep your attention there as much and as long as possible, it will anchor you in the now.

A third tip for getting present involves fully utilizing all your senses. Imagine how present you would have to be if you were riding blindfolded. Taking away one sense heightens others which requires us to sink more into our body. Rather than think your way through a run, it's ideal to FEEL with bodily awareness and presence, and it's all done in the moment.

The biggest indicators to whether you spend time living in the moment or not occur when you're presented with major, or even minor life challenges. In times like this, can you step back and witness your thoughts or do your emotions completely take over and control you?

When something happens that "isn't supposed to," let it pass through you without hitting a wall of mental resistance, as if you're invisible. In doing so, you can focus on positive thoughts, and look for the lesson and the gift, rather than allowing emotions to overwhelm you, giving you the ability to handle any crisis with less stress and greater ease.

> *People are like stained-glass windows. They sparkle and shine when the sun is out, but when the darkness sets in, their true beauty is revealed only if there is a light from within.*

- Elisabeth Kubler-Ross

PRACTICES

I've written quite a bit about developing a baseline foundation of confidence that never wavers, but if we forget where that comes from, and we don't nurture certain relationships, or we allow negative forces from the outside to overwhelm us, our confidence level CAN go down the tubes.

Understanding this, I've taken it upon myself to develop regular practices and certain ways of being that have become habits. I encourage you to establish similar habits, and hope that doing so will be as helpful to you as it's been to me.

When I first developed these practices, my confidence level wasn't real high. In large part, because I've continued them regardless of how good I'm feeling (and I especially continue them when life gets hectic), my confidence continues to grow.

Even if we get off track a bit, a baseline level of confidence is likely to remain, but it's not a chance I want to take. Just like going to the gym once won't get you and keep you fit, we have to keep flexing and building our confidence muscles. This isn't a sign of weakness. There's no shame in structuring our lives in ways that help us to stay mentally and emotionally strong. After all, we are all constantly bombarded with things in life that have potential to knock us off track. Being purposeful and proactive about your daily habits can make all the difference.

These little practices or rituals may resonate with you or inspire you to create your own. Or, you may even question what they have to do with confidence? The truth is, the little every day habits and ways of being we develop have everything to do with the confidence we have when we arrive at the barrel race.

They are investments in the relationships to "source & self." These practices are additional ways in which we can add to our foundational level of confidence by helping us FEEL GOOD about ourselves.

Years ago, I wouldn't have understood the importance of establishing these habits, and I certainly wouldn't have thought it was realistic to think I "had time" in my busy schedule for them. Now, I believe that I can't afford NOT to make these rituals part of my life. I don't believe in doing anything half way, and the purpose I was put on this Earth to fulfill requires me to be at my very best.

> *"You should sit in meditation for twenty minutes every day — unless you're too busy. Then you should sit for an hour."*
> **- Zen proverb**

Self-Care

The better you take care of YOU, the better you'll be able to show up to the people and things you value the most. Think of your self-care practices as part of the foundation of a house – your inner home. To step out and shine in any arena of life requires a solid inner foundation, the practices below help build that.

- Just like a good run starts in the alley, a good day starts with a good morning, and a good morning, starts with a good night of sleep. Make it a priority to get it - you'll be less cranky in the morning and more ready to attack the day with a positive attitude!
- Unhealthy food choices create brain fog, fatigue, mood swings, and weaken our immune system. It's so worth the extra time it takes to plan ahead and nourish your body in ways that create long lasting energy, and mental clarity.
- When you make movement an everyday priority, you are making an investment in your physical and mental health. On days you don't get a workout from riding or doing chores, choose activities that you enjoy and will follow through with on a regular basis.
- Steer clear of activities or environments that tend to bring up negative feelings. Avoid over-indulging in food, drink, gossip or anything that will leave you feeling slimy, bad or regretful. Make it your goal to

spend your time doing things that build your feelings of worth, rather than lower them.

- We can choose to spend our time in ways that add to our life, in ways that are neutral, or in ways that detract from our life. Keep this idea in mind when it comes to television, radio, the internet and news, etc.
- Remind yourself to be present and utilize all your senses, such as the visual splendor of a sunrise, the feel of crisp morning air, the sound of your horse's soft nicker, a warm hug from a friend, or even the softness of your cat's fur.

Nurture Relationships

When it comes right down to what is most important in life – relationships are at the top of the list. As humans, we have a need for relating and connecting to others. Honor this by setting aside time to nurture, develop and enjoy your relationships to source, self, as well as your beloved family & friends.

- Each morning I recommend spending at least 10 minutes in quiet meditation and/or prayer, as well as dedicating time to uplifting reading. For me, this is time to get mentally and emotionally grounded, which is so helpful for setting ourselves up to handle any challenges the day presents.
- Each week set aside special "dates" with your significant other or loved ones. Enjoy this special one on one time by making a point to share what you've been learning in regards to life or your relationships. Exchange compliments with each other. This leaves both parties feeling good and appreciated.
- Once a week, set aside a couple hours to do something special for yourself without interruptions. You might explore some scenic, beautiful country on a relaxing trail ride, or take a long, hot bath. Taking this time to recharge allows you to show up at your best in the world.
- Nurture relationships with family and friends through keeping in touch with them regularly, and scheduling

lunch dates or visits. Connecting with others is vital for every person's mental and emotional wellbeing, but especially for women.

- When it comes to building relationships, keep tabs not only on your thoughts, but also choose your words carefully. Words carry energy to attract what we want or don't want for ourselves and others. Always choose to communicate with complete openness, honesty and integrity.
- Remember you set the standards for how others treat you by how you treat yourself. You may need to preserve your own well-being by choosing not to spend time with certain people, but remember, their outer projections are a reflection of the confidence and love they are missing in their own inner foundation.

Fuel Your Passion

It IS possible to achieve success in the world of tough competition without being cutthroat and ruthless. The WAY we go about reaching our barrel racing goals is important. I'm fiercely determined and aggressive when the need arises, but this strength is sourced from a foundation of trust, love and acceptance.

- Schedule time every day to spend working toward your horsemanship and barrel racing goals. If you don't ride, you might read or watch training DVD's. Make a committed decision to consistently put in the time it takes for your barrel racing dreams to materialize.
- Take pride in your horses and the physical belongings that you've invested in. When you take good care of your horses, vehicles, and equipment they are more likely to take good care of you.
- Prepare appropriately for competition, but at the same time loosen your grip on the outcome. When you don't achieve some goal you had your sights on, love and accept yourself unconditionally regardless. Accept your results, then look for the lesson and recalibrate with enthusiasm to try again.

- Allow your horses to continue teaching you the value of being present. They live in the moment 24/7 and are great reminders that we will be most successful when we join them in the NOW.
- Check comparison and judgment at the door. In barrel racing, your competition can be your greatest support system. Make a point to compliment and lift each other up. Cheerfulness is contagious, don't just catch it – spread it to others!
- Rather than complain about something you're not happy with, take action to change it or pray that your perception of the problem be changed. The more you talk and think about what you don't like, the more of it you attract into your life. Make a point to talk more about your joys than your pain.

> **You have to be able to center yourself, to let all of your emotions go. Don't ever forget that you play with your soul as well as your body.**
>
> **- Kareem Abdul-Jabbar**

TIPS FOR COMPETITION

As you can see, so much of what we do to develop and maintain confidence happens well before we arrive at a venue to compete. I believe we should place focus on developing an unwavering foundation of confidence, but when the stakes are high, it also helps to have an additional layer, "frosting on the cake" so to speak.

We all source that additional confidence in differing ways. Maybe you feel extra confident when you're very well prepared, some people on the other hand can confidently fly by the seat of their pants and achieve positive results. Maybe listening to uplifting music helps, or warming up in a quiet, secluded area if possible. Figure out what it is specifically that YOU can do in advance to up YOUR feelings of confidence at the barrel race – and DO THEM!

Below are some additional tips that might be helpful in those moments before you make a run, when the pressure is on and you may be subjected to feelings of self-doubt.

Confidence Affirmations

Utilizing affirmations wasn't one of those things I took seriously until it was recommended to me from a number of trusted sources. Affirmations are indeed valuable in the same way that repetition is valuable for teaching our horses. If you repeat something enough times, as long as there is a foundation of understanding in place, eventually it will stick.

I recommend you make a list of affirmations that when reminded of, inspire positive feelings and bring you confidence. You might post quotes or inspirational one liners on your bathroom mirror, fridge or in the tack room of your horse trailer. Also keep a list in your boot bag so you can refer to it in an instant, even moments before you go in the arena. You might include…

- Certain accomplishments you have achieved with your horse(s), describe how it felt.
- Positive qualities that your horse has that make him a winner (list them ALL).
- Positive qualities that you have that make you a winner - don't hold back!
- A written reminder of what you need to focus on right now (riding, your run, your horse).
- Any other positive, refreshing words that specifically bring confidence to YOU (remember to write in terms of what you want or have, rather than what you *don't* want/have).

Some Examples…

"My environment does not affect me, I radiate with powerful, positive, confidence."

"Even though competing puts me outside my comfort zone, I choose to enjoy myself and have fun."

"I choose to keep self-talk confidence-enhancing, everything else is blocked out."

"I am in control of my thoughts, and I chose to focus on myself, my horse and our performance."

"I am prepared, flexible and can adapt with patience and flexibility to any change, challenge or adversity."

"I have done my best to prepare and will turn over the results to a power greater than myself."

"There will be things I cannot change about competition, but I always choose a positive attitude and perception."

"I choose to stand straight, ride tall and exude confidence in competition."

"I compete only with the clock. My goal is to be better than I was yesterday."

"I have confidence in my abilities, yet am humble and grateful."
"My best is *always* enough."
"I am focused and ready to compete to the best of my ability."
"I commit to striving for perfection, but accept that I can't always achieve it."
"I will trust my horse, trust our training, and trust our preparation."
"I was born to do this!"

Gratitude Bath

Taking a bath isn't likely to be what's on your mind in those moments in the warm-up pen before your run. However, immersing yourself completely in gratitude can be a great way to block out any self-doubt and only focus on the good.

- Consider how fortunate you are to be able-bodied and minded, which makes it possible for you to ride horses and pursue your dreams in the sport of barrel racing. Celebrate the fact that you are present with your horse, ready to have *fun!*
- Think thoughts of gratitude and appreciation for your amazing equine partners and their selfless cooperation that allows you to do what you love.
- Become mindful of the people you love and appreciate in your life. Think of your loved ones, and all the things they do and ways they support you and your barrel racing.
- Remind yourself how grateful and appreciative you'll be when you exit the arena after an amazing run. When you create the feeling you want to have *after the run,* it becomes more likely to be your reality.

*See the "Inner Game" chapter of *Secrets to Barrel Racing Success*, and the "Winning Warm-up" chapter of *The First 51 Barrel Racing Exercises to Develop a Champion* for even more pointers for mental pre-run preparation.

> **Courage is not the absence of fear, it is the willingness to step through it.**
>
> **- Unknown**

CONFIDENCE SMASHERS

When Outer Influences
Threaten Your Inner Foundation

If you've been barrel racing long enough, you may have had some experiences, even repetitive experiences that weren't too positive and did a number on your confidence. Maybe your current horse has been known to duck out and run up the fence, or bust in two after leaving the third barrel, or maybe you had some close calls with a past horse that reared at the gate. Perhaps you actually had an accident and suffered a severe injury that now causes you to mentally "safety up." Maybe you've just been flat embarrassed in public and now have a deep fear of what others think. Or perhaps you were crazy confident as a horseback kid and are now at mid-life wondering where that fearlessness went?

Maybe you have a confidence-killing person in your life - someone whose presence seems to lower your self-worth. They might come right out and say or do things with the intent to hurt you. Their own weak inner foundation may show up as subtle manipulation to keep you down on their level.

In both of these cases, when legitimate outside sources have damaged your confidence, the first step toward restoring it, is stopping the cycle. That means determining whether you have good reason to feel unconfident or whether your fear is irrational or coming from the past.

As you determine where the loss in confidence is actually coming from, proceed with caution. It's always easy to point the finger and assume that it's something on the outside that is the culprit, when that is not always the case.

Sometimes, our own "imaginary" fear creates legitimate issues with people and horses that didn't even existent initially.

Our own insecurities can cause those around us to align with how we feel, making it seem as though our horse *is not* worthy of confidence, or that others really *are* saying, doing and behaving in ways that are intentionally damaging our self-worth.

If you keep competing on a horse that is actually dangerous, or has gone a mile by the first barrel for the 100th time, by all means – STOP! STOP repeating the confidence draining cycle. The same goes for people you are absolutely certain are saying and doing things to put you down. Your confidence is soooo precious, you must take a stand for yourself and preserve and protect it with the greatest of care.

Once you've put the brakes on whatever is causing your confidence level to drop, dig even deeper within to ask yourself – what action must I take to turn this around?

It might mean selling your horse, it might mean getting professional help with your horse, it might mean reading the books in the resource section, it might mean having an open, honest conversation with someone about how you feel, it might mean setting boundaries with that person, or it might mean making a decision to excuse them from your life completely.

> *"Life is too short to spend your precious time trying to convince a person who wants to live in gloom and doom otherwise. Give lifting that person your best show, but don't hang around long enough for his or her bad attitude to pull you down. Instead, surround yourself with optimistic people."*
> **- Zig Ziglar**

If you realize that the fear and self-doubt you experience is indeed irrational, for example if you safety up all the way to the first barrel for fear that you'll go by, based on your past experience with another horse, or your own thinking errors turn around what other people say and do, so that it's interpreted as something negative, when in fact it's not intended that way, then it's time to do your *own work.* That's where the contents of this book come into play.

Overcoming a genuine fear issue with a (safe) horse, means stretching outside your comfort zone just a little at a time. Just like with horses, if we are forced into something we aren't ready for, we risk creating *even more* of a confidence issue than we started with.

Little by little, make it your goal to overcome any fear issues in baby steps. Celebrate each little milestone and love and accept yourself in the process. Surround yourself with understanding and supportive people. Be mindful that fear in us can contribute to the development of fear issues in our horses.

You're not the only one who is affected by thinking errors. Let this reminder serve as motivation, but not pressure. Implement and utilize the suggestions in this guide and other resources to develop a more positive, realistic perspective.

You can also focus on all the ways in which you can develop your confidence across the board and it will benefit you with horses. If you've had close calls with dangerous horses, get yourself the sanest, safest horse you can find. If it's speed or losing control you fear,

> *"I have not ceased being fearful, but I have ceased to let fear control me."*
> - Erica Jong

practice opening up and letting go on a four wheeler or even ride a roller coaster. If being ejected from the saddle is what you fear, build your balance, strength and stability with a good fitness program and be sure you're getting TONS of riding time in. Turn your discomfort zone into your comfort zone.

Build your confidence in general by utilizing and expanding on what I've shared in this book and doing your inner homework, but also focus in on the very specific ways in that you can develop outer confidence based in your individual situation.

Most importantly, remember that our past experiences cannot hold us back, it's what we do with those experiences mentally and emotionally in the *here and now* that create roadblocks.

Even if limited thinking has held you back for years, know that every single moment brings opportunity to make a new choice.

The **success you desire** is not *just possible,* it's *waiting for you* to GET ON and GO!

> **With confidence,
> you have won before
> you have started.**

- Marcus Garvey

IN SUMMARY

I've shared the danger and risks of competition when it comes to developing confidence, the importance of establishing an inner foundation, where I believe that stems from, how to develop it through two very special relationships, the meaning, value of, and suggestions for being in the moment, as well as additional techniques and practices for maintaining and continuing to expand your level of confidence.

Remember that all this requires continuous effort on your part. There are outer influences that *can and will* tear you down, IF you allow them to. If you do find yourself feeling unconfident, refer to this book and remember that *you can always change those feelings.* You can always take time to nurture those important relationships, better develop your own foundation, simply spend time in the moment, try on a new perspective, or choose a better-feeling thought.

As you regain clarity, I hope you truly see yourself as if you were looking through the loving eyes of God, and that as you do, you're reminded of what you may have forgotten – that in the arena, and in life, you *always have been*, and always *will be* ENOUGH.

> *Your horse will only be as brave as you are.*

- Unknown

THE CONFIDENT HORSE

While hauling lots of miles and competing can play a part in building confidence, I'm sure you realize that there's so much more to the confidence building process for horses than just jumping them in and out of the trailer repetitively, pounding the pavement, and exposing them to the sights and sounds of rodeo road.

This guide has gone in great depth to describe ways in which we, as barrel racers can develop confidence in ourselves. Horses feed off our energy, emotions and thoughts. Often they know what we are thinking and feeling, even before we do.

If you hold back in any way, or are tentative, on some level, your horse will mirror you. A lack of confidence in yourself can show up as subtle hesitation and/or issues with timing in a run. At the deepest level, a lack of confidence is essentially fear, and fear slows everything down, perhaps by only a barely noticeable, narrow margin – but in our sport, we must become aware and work toward closing *all* existing gaps. You'll be amazed at how effective increasing your own confidence will be for your horse, as well as improving your riding and timing in a run.

There's even more we can do to help our horses in the area of confidence. This starts with first really understanding more about the trust they must have in us to absolutely give their all on the pattern.

What if someone came up to you, said they were going to put a bit in your mouth (one of the most sensitive parts of your body) and lead you around with it? Would you trust them?

Again, I'll share a definition of confidence…

> *"The feeling or belief that one can rely on someone or something; firm trust… the state of feeling certain about the truth of something."*

Horses can gain or lose confidence in several areas, including their rider, as a learner, in their environment, and with other horses. When they are completely confident in YOU, you can help them be confident in all other areas.

At BarrelRacingTips.com and in my books, I've written about the relationship between horse and rider, and how critical it is that we provide appropriate leadership to our horses. Horses are wired mentally to do what they feel is necessary to feel OK about things. Developing a confident horse has a lot to do with understanding horse psychology and developing our ability to use techniques that work *with* rather than against their natural instincts and BE a person that causes our horses to feel safe.

We need to provide firm leadership, but trying to force a horse to do something they genuinely feel is dangerous, haven't been educated to understand, or simply are not emotionally fit and mature enough to handle, is one of the quickest ways to diminish their confidence. Scaring or threatening them into responding is another. Many timed event speed horses especially are simply running away from and reacting pressure, not responding to it. A horse who is motivated by desire will always outshine one whose performance is based on avoidance. This foundation of trust is built in the little every day interactions with our horses at home and tested in more stressful environments. Any time a horse is distracted or behaves differently in certain environments, it essentially means some aspect of their educational and emotional foundation is not firm enough – we missed the subtle signs and failed to develop it well enough.

While there is a time and place to be firm and effective, force and fear simply aren't necessary when quality leadership and education are in place.

Both of these things, as well as flexibility with training timelines, are crucial for creating confident, willing partners. Remember in the end that horses will always "run faster and jump higher out of heart and desire" vs. fear and intimidation.

There are resources that exist today that offer opportunities to learn how to understand horses as individuals, which can empower us to develop each horse in a way that brings out the very best in each one based on their varying personality characteristics.

To sum it up, when your horse is truly *educated*, you've provided appropriate *leadership*, and self-doubt isn't holding *YOU* back, then the confidence that comes from within yourself and your equine partners as a result is bound to be reflected on the outside in the form of fast times on the pattern.

If developing specific strategies to bring out the very best in your individual horses is something that interests you, I encourage you to stay in contact with me and seek out more learning opportunities and resources on the subject of "equine sports psychology" available at www.BarrelRacingTips.com, as this is a subject I intend to expand on into the future.

> *When every physical and mental resource is focused, one's power to solve a problem multiplies tremendously.*

- Norman Vincent Peale

ADDITIONAL RESOURCES

Books
(For even more suggested reading material visit the Resources page at BarrelRacingTips.com).
- "Do You Think I'm Beautiful" by Angela Thomas
- "A Return to Love" by Marianne Williamson
- "Inside Your Ride" by Tonya Johnston
- "Learned Optimism" by Martin Seligman
- "The Way of the Peaceful Warrior" by Dan Millman
- "The Inner Game of Tennis" by W. Timothy Gallwey
- "The Power of Now" by Eckhart Tolle
- "Zen Mind, Zen Horse" by Alan J. Hamilton, M.D.
- "With Winning in Mind" by Lanny Bassham

Personal Development Programs
- Brené Brown's Gifts of Imperfection e-Course
- Inner Mean Girl Reform School
- Brave Girls Club

Articles + Videos at BarrelRacingTips.com
- In Search of SPEED – How to BE Explosive on the Barrel Pattern!
- FREE Your Barrel Horse from Emotions that Hold Back Athletic Potential
- How to Give Up Micromanaging and GAIN a Horse that LOVES Barrel Racing!
- Let LOVE Overflow for Greater Peace, Joy & Barrel Racing Success
- Freedom to RUN – How to Prevent Perfectionism from Slowing You Down
- Meditation – Beneficial to Barrel Racers?
- Provide Motivation and Create Consistency in the Barrel Horse

*To grow, you must be willing
to let your present and future
be totally unlike your past.
Your history is not your destiny.*

- Alan Cohen

ABOUT THE AUTHOR

Little did she know where such humble beginnings would lead. Today Heather Smith is living her dream. She can be found in the arena developing her barrel horses, on the road competing with them and sharing what she's learned with others, *or* in her home office writing about it all!

Over the years, Heather has overcome numerous obstacles that stood in the way of barrel racing success. Lessons were often hard earned, which is why she is enthusiastic to pave a smoother path for other barrel racers. Although she has successfully trained for and competed in reining events, and has experience with colt starting and rehabilitating troubled horses, barrel racing continues to be Heather's primary focus.

Perhaps what sets Heather apart is her unbridled enthusiasm for learning. This passion has inspired her to create and take advantage of opportunities to learn from the best in the industry. Heather has worked closely and ridden with many leading professionals, whose guidance has no doubt influenced and shaped her integrative style of horsemanship and teaching.

In addition, Heather has invested a great deal of time and resources developing her education on the specific topics of equine massage, chiropractic, nutrition and natural hoof care. She holds an Associate of Applied Science Degree in Veterinary Technology and maintains licensure as a Veterinary Technician.

Heather's experiences have led her to realize that achieving success in barrel racing, or any discipline, is really more about personal development than horse training, and that only when we reveal the best in ourselves, can we do the same with horses.

Through her own experiences, she's become determined to make the critical but lesser-known *secrets to barrel racing success* more understandable and readily available to barrel racers around the world.

Today, she does just that through her web site – www.BarrelRacingTips.com – where she offers quality, original how-to articles and Q&A videos as well as a collection of resources designed specifically for barrel racers who are ready and willing to take their competition to the next level.

A North Dakota native, Heather spent fourteen years in Wyoming before she and her husband Craig became Texans in 2013. They make their home in central Texas between Waco and College Station.

Be sure to visit www.BarrelRacingTips.com to receive free winning tips and stay updated on opportunities to learn from Heather.

For even more barrel racing tips and encouragement, connect on Facebook at www.Facebook.com/BarrelRacingTips.

Made in the USA
Monee, IL
06 June 2022

97545170R00046